GEN
1

RICHARD PONTEFRACT

WESTBOW
PRESS®
A DIVISION OF THOMAS NELSON
& ZONDERVAN

WestBow Press books may be ordered through booksellers or by contacting:

WestBow Press
A Division of Thomas Nelson & Zondervan
1663 Liberty Drive
Bloomington, IN 47403
www.westbowpress.com
844-714-3454

Scripture marked (NKJV) taken from the New King James Version®. Copyright © 1982 by Thomas Nelson. Used by permission. All rights reserved.

Scripture marked (KJV) taken from the King James Version of the Bible.

ISBN: 978-1-6642-2806-1 (sc)
ISBN: 978-1-6642-2805-4 (e)

Print information available on the last page.

WestBow Press rev. date: 03/24/2021

Prelude

This is for all those who are unable to find the time to actually read the entire Bible.

I've done it for you and condensed the plot into a 1-hour read.

Hope you enjoy!

PunkerPirate

8-5-2013

After 30 plus years of dwelling and debating on it all, this is my attempt to logically explain what and why I believe regarding Christianity having actually read the entire story, front to back, 3 times. Me in a *nut*shell, 53, born into a Christian family, mother very devout, but mentally distraught and emotionally unstable to the point of being extremely offensive to any and all she might meet. Having been dragged to many a church of various denominations during my youth, the turmoil within the family left me with disdain for my mother and Christianity. I guess I was 20 or so when I finally had enough and just flat out told her...

"NO, I DO NOT BELIEVE"!!!

Her cry at that moment was:

"JUST READ THE STORY"!!!

Of which I replied:

"OK!!! I WILL READ THE STORY!!!

Yes, I was angry!!!

And I did read the story...

The 1st time as a complete non-believer with no pre-conceived notions or beliefs, for I never paid any attention to anything they were trying to tell me. However, by the time I had finished "The Story"

I came to believe and walked that aisle to give my life to the.

"LORD JESUS CHRIST" at Rehoboth Baptist in Tucker, Georgia.

Please note I simply read the story. I did not try and memorize scripture & verse for I was not able to do so and comprehend what it had to say. Nor did I read or pay any attention to any commentaries or footnotes. The 1st

Bible I read was Concordance, simply because it was there at the time, the 2nd being King James and the 3rd New Revised Standard.

Second time after having come amongst the brethren. Baptist mainly, and discovering that much of what I had thought I had come to know and understand simply by reading God's word was unheard of...

Now being of sound mind and body I said to myself.

"Surely I had not missed all that"?

And went back to reading that story again, this time with the King...

The 3rd time having convinced myself I am not the ***nut they think I am,*** and I am going to confirm this to myself one more time.

The biggest difference in my understanding is I have taken the Bible literally. It meant to me exactly what it said. Parables are noted in the Bible as such and metaphors are easily discernible such as when Christ says

"I am the door"

John 10:9 KJV

I am the door: by me if any man enter in, he shall be saved, and shall go in and out, and find pasture.

Notice he did not say "a door" for he is neither "a door", nor is there any other way to enter salvation.

Whenever I hear "I have the (Holy Spirit), and what that says is not what that means"

My jaw's wide open :o

I'm not biting!

My beliefs here within are not necessarily mine conceived by me only, but I have listened throughout the years to what everyone has had to say from all denominations and have taken what has made the most logical sense compared against what I had read and saw to begin with.

Thus, here it goes…

Times New Roman w/14 Font = My Specific Beliefs

Times New Roman w/12 Font = Passages & Scripture Direct from the Bible <u>with my own underlining of what I wish for you to pay most attention to.</u>

Times New Roman w/10 Font = My Writings/Opinions

God was not "All Knowing". While God does know the future and the story is going to end just as it is told, the concept that he was "All Knowing" and the way things are and are going to be was the intent to begin with I find worth dwelling on with question.

God is in control. God was not "All Knowing", or I would consider it "Predestination" and that lends to the perception of a cruel God to say the least. Hell's flames are no joke and there must be some justification for eternal torment for those who end up there other than because it was Gods will.

You cannot logically separate the two, an "All Knowing God" and Predestination.

God has said that he tempts no man.

Nor

Did he intentionally (knowingly) create some 3rd party to do the dirty work for him.

I fail to see how that would be a holy & just God.

James 1:13 KJV

[13]Let no man say when he is tempted, I am tempted of God: for God cannot be tempted with evil, <u>neither tempteth he any man</u>:

I like to reference the end of the story and must ask; you mean to tell me that Satan's just reward is eternal banishment down some flaming bottomless pit for simply obeying God, whose purpose for his creation was to tempt and deceive man. That was God's divine plan? This from a holy, righteous God? My logical mind wants to think that Satan's punishment is due to a coup attempt in the kingdom of God; one God did not foresee or plan on, one that possibly had a chance of succeeding. Now hell's flame makes sense and would be a divine judgment from a just & righteous God.

Some have looked at me and remarked "You can't use logic. God is not logical"

Really?!

We were created in "<u>His Image</u>", yes? Remove from your mind all you were taught before you ever even read <u>a</u> Bible if you have read one at all. Even if you have you have piecemealed it by skipping all around. There is something to be said for taking the Scriptures in the order it was presented and going front to back. I do not see how anyone could understand the plot like that. You do not read any other book or novel like that do you? with any expectations of being able to comprehend the plot...

Start at the beginning and read it in the order God had it assembled.

I consider Romans 9, passages referenced by those who back predestination theology, a generalization of scripture as it relates to any other religion or all those that do not have Christ as the center of its or their theology. It is not an indication of specific individuals predestined to heaven or hell for God said,

"Who so ever"

and since we must assume that His word does not conflict than I look for the logical answer that will encompass all God has had to say on the issue and can make some sense without the conflict and thereby all scripture equaling true.

Below will be passages/verses to support my beliefs taken mostly from the **New King James Bible, (NKJV and/or KJV)** not that it is my favorite but simply because that is what most Protestant denominations wish to reference.

Genesis 2:18 NKJV

[18] And the LORD God said, "*It is* not good that man should be alone; I will make him a helper comparable to him." [19] Out of the ground the LORD God formed every beast of the field and every bird of the air and brought *them* to Adam <u>to see</u> what he would call them. And whatever Adam called each living creature that *was* its name. [20] So Adam gave names to all cattle, to the birds of the air, and to every beast of the field. But for Adam there was not found a helper comparable to him.

Genesis 3:9 NKJV

Then the LORD God called to Adam and said to him, "<u>Where *are* you</u>?"

Genesis 3:13 NKJV

And the Lord God said to the woman, "<u>What is this you have done?</u>" The woman said, "The serpent deceived me, and I ate."

Genesis 4:10 NKJV

And He said, "<u>What have you done</u>? The voice of your brother's blood cries out to me from the ground. [11] So now you *are* cursed from the earth, which has opened its mouth to receive your brother's blood from your hand. ¹² When you till the ground, it shall no longer yield its strength to you. A fugitive and a vagabond you shall be on the earth."

Genesis 6:5 NKJV

⁵ Then the LORD[b] saw that the wickedness of man *was* great in the earth, and *that* every intent of the thoughts of his heart *was* only evil continually. ⁶ And the LORD was sorry that He had made man on the earth, and He was grieved in His heart. ⁷ So the LORD said, "I will destroy man whom I have created from the face of the earth, both man and beast, creeping thing and birds of the air, for I am sorry that I have made them." ⁸ But Noah found grace in the eyes of the LORD.

I will agree that the questions by God above can be perceived as rhetorical, however I just cannot help but ask…

You mean to tell me God knew he would be sorry?

Genesis 11:5 NKJV

But the Lord came down to see the city and the tower which the sons of men had built.

Genesis 18:16 NKJV

¹⁶ Then the men rose from there and looked toward Sodom, and Abraham went with them to send them on the way. ¹⁷ And the LORD said, "Shall I hide from Abraham what I am doing, ¹⁸ since Abraham shall surely become a great and mighty nation, and all the nations of the earth shall be blessed in him? ¹⁹ For I have known him, in order that he may command

his children and his household after him, that they keep the way of the LORD, to do righteousness and justice, that the LORD may bring to Abraham what He has spoken to him." ²⁰ And the LORD said, "Because the outcry against Sodom and Gomorrah is great, and because their sin is very grave, <u>[21]I will go down now and see</u> whether they have done altogether according to the outcry against it that has come to me; <u>and if not, I will know.</u>"

Genesis 22:1 NKJV

Now it came to pass after these things that <u>God tested Abraham,</u> and said to him, "Abraham!" And he said, "Here I am."

GENESIS 22:12 NKJV

¹² And He said, "Do not lay your hand on the lad, or do anything to him; <u>for now, I know</u> that you fear God, since you have not withheld your son, your only *son,* from me."

¹⁵ Then the Angel of the LORD called to Abraham a second time out of heaven, ¹⁶ and said: "By Myself I have sworn, says the LORD, <u>because</u> you have done this thing, and have not withheld your son, your only *son*— ¹⁷ blessing I will bless you, and multiplying I will multiply your descendants as the stars of the heaven and as the sand which *is* on the seashore; and your descendants shall possess the gate of their enemies. ¹⁸ In your seed all the nations of the earth shall be blessed, because you have obeyed my voice." ¹⁹ So Abraham returned to his young men, and they rose and went together to Beersheba; and Abraham dwelt at Beersheba.

Genesis 32:24 NKJV

24 Then Jacob was left alone; and a Man wrestled with him until the breaking of day. 25 Now when he saw that He did not prevail against him, He touched the socket of his hip; and the socket of Jacob's hip was out of joint as He wrestled with him. 26 And He said, "Let Me go, for the day breaks."

Numbers 14:11 NKJV

Then the Lord said to Moses: "How long will these people reject me? And how long will they not believe me, with all the signs which I have performed among them?

Deuteronomy 8:2 NKJV

And you shall remember that the Lord your God led you all the way these forty years in the wilderness, to humble you _and_ test you, to know what _was_ in your heart, whether you would keep His commandments or not.

Deuteronomy 9:14 NKJV

Let Me alone, that I may destroy them and blot out their name from under heaven; and I will make of you a nation mightier and greater than they.'

I read that and say to myself "He's really angry here!", and remain totally befuddled,

Pondering as to why that would have been the plan...?

And by the time I had finished the book of Genesis (the 1ˢᵗ **Book** of the Bible), and even if I had had the perception of an "All Knowing God" to begin with, the perception of such was completely wiped out of my mind and never to return. It seems to be the opinion of most that if you do not believe God was not all knowing that you do not honor God as you should or that would mean God is not sovereign. I submit that it is you who dishonors God by not taking him <u>exactly</u> at his own word.

You create an image of God to the complete unbeliever as some cruel entity whom most wish nothing to do with. Being "Sovereign" does not necessarily mean that you do not have to fight for it. The word is used quite often throughout the Bible (<u>except King James</u>) about the kings of Israel who fought to be "Sovereign".

1 Kings 4:21 KJV

²¹And Solomon reigned over all kingdoms from the river unto the land of the Philistines, and unto the border of Egypt: they brought presents and served Solomon all the days of his life.

The King James along with others does not even use the word "Sovereign", neither for God nor man. You find it in the author's pre/post-verse footnotes. Other versions of the Bible do use the word. Some for God and man, some for God only. It is thought provoking to consider what the impact of the word "Sovereign", has on one's mind and what they believe and then enlightening to see the mass confusion that causes. The same holds true for the word "Omnipotent". It is used in one verse of one Bible Translation,

King James

When you think about it, there are many words of the English Language of consequential impact on what one perceives and when there are so many versions of the Bible with each author utilizing whatever choice of words, they like best, mass confusion is easy to understand. Hades is another good example. Early versions of the Bible seem to indicate a place of holding where all the dead went before Christ. Newer revisions like King James indicate Hades is simply another word for Hell.

And is no wonder why everyone has their hands in the air crying out…

"We're just not meant to understand the mind of God!"

Revelation 19:6 (found only in <u>King James, KJV and/or NKJV</u>)

And I heard as it were the voice of a great multitude, and as the voice of many waters, and as the voice of mighty thundering, saying, alleluia: for the Lord God <u>omnipotent</u> reigneth.

The Trinity is 3 separate entities of equal power coming together in mutual agreement to form the One God Head.

Genesis 1:26 NKJV

[26] Then God said, "Let <u>Us</u> make man in our image, according to our likeness; let them have dominion over the fish of the sea, over the birds of the air, and over the cattle, over all[b] the earth and over every creeping thing that creeps on the earth."

Genesis 3:22 KJV

"And the LORD God said, Behold, the man is become as <u>one of us</u>, to know good and evil: and now, lest he put forth his hand, and take also of the tree of life, and eat, and live forever:"

Genesis 11:5 NKJV

[5] But the LORD came down to see the city and the tower which the sons of men had built. [6] And the LORD said, "Indeed the people *are* one and they all have one language, and this is what they begin to do; now nothing that they propose to do will be withheld from them. [7] Come, <u>let Us</u> go down and there confuse their language, that they may not understand one another's speech." [8] So the LORD scattered them abroad from there over

the face of all the earth, and they ceased building the city. ⁹ Therefore its name is called Babel, because there the LORD confused the language of all the earth; and from there the LORD scattered them abroad over the face of all the earth.

Mark 13:32 NKJV

"But of that day and hour no one knows, not even the angels in heaven, nor the Son, but only the Father.

If God was one entity taking on 3 separate personalities this part about Christ not knowing the day or hour is beyond comprehension.

Philippians 2:6 NKJV

who, being in the form of God, did not consider it robbery to be equal with God,

Creation was longer than 6/24-hour periods and most likely each day was a thousand years.

Genesis 2:4 NKJV

This *is* the history[a] of the heavens and the earth when they were created, in the day that the LORD God made the earth and the heavens, ⁵ before any plant of the field was in the earth and before any herb of the field had grown. For the LORD God had not caused it to rain on the earth, and *there was* no man to till the ground; ⁶ but a mist went up from the earth and watered the whole face of the ground.

My perception of the above passages is that God set up in his creation the design of all living things to reproduce and then let time take its course.

God is not hanging around involved in the direct real time creation of every flower that blossoms or every child born. Those offended by this concept want to imply that you are backing evolution or that if God did not make it all come about within the time frame, they have allotted God is just not God enough for them. God is God enough for me and I do not care what kind of timeline it took.

But each day was in fact 1000 years is making the most logical sense.

Genesis 2:18 NKJV

[18] And the LORD God said, "*It is* not good that man should be alone; I will make him a helper comparable to him." [19] Out of the ground the LORD God formed every beast of the field and every bird of the air and brought *them* to Adam to see what he would call them. And whatever Adam called each living creature that *was* its name. [20] So Adam gave names to all cattle, to the birds of the air, and to every beast of the field. But for Adam there was not found a helper comparable to him.[21] And the LORD God caused a deep sleep to fall on Adam, and he slept; and He took one of his ribs and closed the flesh in its place. [22] Then the rib which the LORD God had taken from man He made into a woman, and He brought her to the man.

So, in less than 24 hours Adam puts names to all the beast of the field and birds of the air and then God puts him to sleep and creates Eve. Really? I just cannot imagine my God having to be in that kind of hurry.

Can you picture the scene with all the creatures in and out in a flash?

"Hurry Adam, Hurry! I have a woman to create and the sun is setting"!

Please!?

He has all of eternity…

If you now want to say,

"Well, there just weren't that many animals at that time"

You now become a supporter of evolution theology.

2 Peter 3:8 NKJV

But, beloved, do not forget this one thing, that with the Lord one day *is* as a thousand years, and a thousand years as one day.

We are created in God's Image. They have a face, a physique and feel the same emotions that have been bestowed upon us.

Genesis 6:6 NKJV

[6] And the LORD was sorry that He had made man on the earth, and He was grieved in His heart. [7] So the LORD said, "I will destroy man whom I have created from the face of the earth, both man and beast, creeping thing and birds of the air, for I am sorry that I have made them." [8] But Noah found grace in the eyes of the LORD.

Genesis 8:20 NKJV

[20] Then Noah built an altar to the LORD AND took of every clean animal and of every clean bird and offered burnt offerings on the altar. [21] And the LORD smelled a soothing aroma. Then the LORD said in His heart, "I will never again curse the ground for man's sake, although the imagination of man's heart *is* evil from his youth; nor will I again destroy every living thing as I have done.

Most assume that much of the Bible is metaphorical. I say <u>all the above means exactly what it says</u> for if it was metaphorical it is open to anyone's interpretation who want to claim the "<u>Holy Spirit</u>". Metaphors are easy to comprehend and if the Lord smelling a "soothing aroma" does not mean exactly what it says, there would be way too many answers to the question,

"What does it mean?"

That the abstract minds of the many various individuals all claiming the "Holy Spirit" could possibly conceive.

Genesis 32:24 NKJV

[24] Then Jacob was left alone; and a Man wrestled with him until the breaking of day. [25] Now when He saw that He did not prevail against him, He touched the socket of his hip; and the socket of Jacob's hip was out of joint as He wrestled with him. [26] And He said, "Let Me go, for the day breaks." But he said, "I will not let you go unless you bless me!"[27] So He said to him, "What *is* your name?" He said, "Jacob." [28] And He said, "Your name shall no longer be called Jacob, but Israel;[b] for you have struggled with God and with men, and have prevailed."

God takes the form of a man and is literally involved in a wrestling match where he was physically losing until taking out Jacobs hip.

I can agree here that God already knew his name and was making a rhetorical question simply to lead to the change of name.

Genesis 32:30 KJV

So, Jacob called the name of the place Peniel: "For I have seen God face to face, and my life is preserved."

Exodus 20:5 NKJV

you shall not bow down to them nor serve them. For I, the Lord your God, *am* a jealous God, visiting the iniquity of the fathers upon the children to the third and fourth *generations* of those who hate me,

Exodus 22:23 NKJV

[23] If you afflict them in any way, *and* they cry at all to me, I will surely hear their cry; [24] and my wrath will become hot, and I will kill you with the sword; your wives shall be widows, and your children fatherless.

Deuteronomy 4:28 NKJV

And there you will serve gods, the work of men's hands, wood, and stone, which neither see nor hear nor eat nor smell.

Deuteronomy 6:15 NKJV

(for the Lord, your God *is* a jealous God among you), lest the anger of the Lord your God be aroused against you and destroy you from the face of the earth.

Amos 5:21 NKJV

"I hate, I despise your feast days, and I do not savor your sacred assemblies.

John 3:16 NKJV

For <u>God so loved</u> the world that He gave His only begotten Son, that whoever believes in Him should not perish but have everlasting life.

John 20:27 NKJV

Then He said to Thomas, "Reach your finger here, and look at my hands; and reach your hand *here and* put *it* into <u>my side</u>. Do not be unbelieving, but believing

Mark 14:25 NKJV

Assuredly, I say to you, I will no longer drink of the fruit of the vine until that day when <u>I drink it new</u> in the kingdom of God."

God has within himself every emotion and physical attribute that has been bestowed upon man. Yes, he even eats and drinks, not for nutrition's sake mind you but for the enjoyment. I have even dwelled on the possibility though not mentioned in the Bible that it was loneliness when God 1st came to the knowledge of…

"<u>I Am that I Am</u>",

His 1st creation, another entity just like himself.

(10/27/2013) God did say in the beginning that it was not good for man to be alone and perhaps it is because he had already known the feeling for himself…

Genesis 2:18 NKJV

And the Lord God said, "*It is* not good that man should be alone; I will make him a helper comparable to him."

God created man of all races at the same time and chose one man and woman of which to establish a personal relationship with, that being Adam and Eve.

Genesis 4:13 NKJV

And Cain said to the LORD, "My punishment *is* greater than I can bear! [14] surely you have driven me out this day from the face of the ground; I shall be hidden from your face; I shall be a fugitive and a vagabond on the earth, and it will happen *that* anyone who finds me will kill me."

[15] And the LORD said to him, "Therefore, [b] whoever kills Cain, vengeance shall be taken on him sevenfold." And the LORD set a mark on Cain, lest anyone finding him should kill him.

Genesis 5:1 NKJV

This is the book of the genealogy of Adam. In the day that God created man, He made him in the likeness of God. [2] He created them male and female and blessed them and called them Mankind in the day they were created. [3] And Adam lived one hundred and thirty years, and begot *a son* in his own likeness, after his image, and named him Seth. [4] After he begot Seth, the days of Adam were eight hundred years; and he had sons and daughters. [5] So all the days that Adam lived were nine hundred and thirty years; and he died

It is not clear how old Cain was when he killed his brother, but it was before the birth of Seth, and Adam was only 130 years old at his birth. Cain was worried about venturing into the world for there would be those out to kill him. It would take a mass amount of childbearing between Adam and Eve along with their children having children as children for there to be a population of people in the territories beyond for Cain to be afraid of. I think had it simply been family he was afraid of; it would have been noted.

I will concede however if all were out to kill him it may very well have been family since they would have all heard about the death of their brother.

And then of course it really does not matter since the entire population was wiped out in the flood and all of humanity started over with Noah and family…

More than one wife was not a sin in the Old Testament, and I am not so sure it is sin now.

If you actually love all your wives and are able to care for all those children. However, if it is lust that has hold of you, then you are in sin or if you are relying on government assistance in any way to care for all those children you should be castrated anyway.

Genesis 25:5 NKJV

[5] And Abraham gave all that he had to Isaac. [6] But Abraham gave gifts to the sons of the <u>concubines</u> which Abraham had; and while he was still living, he sent them eastward, away from Isaac his son, to the country of the east.

I am unable to rationalize how the very same man could drag his own son up the mountain with the intent to slay him because that is what God told him to do yet unable to control his desires for an endless family if in fact God had told him it was forbidden. I have heard others say Abraham may have had as many as 75 concubines.

Genesis 26:34 NKJV

When Esau was forty years old, he took as wives Judith the daughter of Beeri the Hittite, and Basemath the daughter of Elon the Hittite.

Genesis 28:9 NKJV

So, Esau went to Ishmael and took Mahalath the daughter of Ishmael, Abraham's son, the sister of Nebajoth, to be his wife in addition to the wives he had.

Genesis 29:31 NKJV

[31] When the LORD saw that Leah *was* unloved, He opened her womb; but Rachel *was* barren. [32] So Leah conceived and bore a son, and she called his name Reuben;[a] for she said, "The LORD has surely looked on my affliction. Now therefore, my husband will love me." [33] Then she conceived again and bore a son, and said, "Because the LORD has heard that I *am* unloved, He has therefore given me this *son* also." And she called his name Simeon.[b] [34] She conceived again and bore a son, and said, "Now this time my husband will become attached to me, because I have borne him three sons." Therefore his name was called Levi.[c] [35] And she conceived again and bore a son, and said, "Now I will praise the LORD." Therefore she called his name Judah.[d] Then she stopped bearing.

Genesis 30:17 NKJV

[17] And God listened to Leah, and she conceived and bore Jacob a fifth son. [18] Leah said, "God has given me my wages, because I have given my maid to my husband." So she called his name Issachar.[f] [19] Then Leah conceived again and bore Jacob a sixth son. [20] And Leah said, "God has endowed me *with* a good endowment; now my husband will dwell with me, because I have borne him six sons." So she called his name Zebulun.[g] [21] Afterward she bore a daughter, and called her name Dinah.

²² Then God remembered Rachel, and God listened to her and opened her womb. ²³ And she conceived and bore a son, and said, "God has taken away my reproach." ²⁴ So she called his name Joseph,[h] and said, "The LORD shall add to me another son."

The above passages show God interacting and blessing both of Jacob's wives

Deuteronomy 21:15 NKJV

¹⁵ "If a man has two wives, the one loved and the other [c] unloved, and *both* the loved and the [d]unloved have borne him sons, if the firstborn son belongs to the [e]unloved, ¹⁶ then it shall be in the day he [f]wills what he has to his sons, he cannot make the son of the loved the firstborn before the son of the [g] unloved, who is the firstborn.

Judges 8:30 NKJV

Now Gideon had seventy sons who were his direct descendants, for he had many wives.

1 Samuel 25:43 NKJV

David had also taken Ahinoam of Jezreel, and they both became his wives.

2 Samuel 5:13 NKJV

Meanwhile David took more concubines and wives from Jerusalem, after he came from Hebron; and more sons and daughters were born to David.

2 Samuel 11:26 NKJV

²⁶ Now when the wife of Uriah heard that Uriah her husband was dead, she mourned for her husband. ²⁷ When the *time of* mourning was over, David sent and ^[j]brought her to his house and she became his wife; then she bore him a son. But the thing that David had done was evil in the sight of the LORD.

2 Samuel 12:7 NKJV

⁷ Nathan then said to David, "You are the man! Thus, says the LORD God of Israel, 'It is I who anointed you king over Israel, and it is I who delivered you from the hand of Saul. ⁸ I also gave you your master's house and your master's wives into your ^[g]care, and I gave you the house of Israel and Judah; and if *that had been* too little, I would have added to you many more things like these!

God was willing to bless David with as many women as he wanted, though I have no idea just what kind of blessing that would be.

It was having a man killed after he would not go lie with his own wife so he could stand guard for David, his King who covered up the adultery and the child that was to be borne by sending Uriah to the front battle line.

That was David's sin.

1 Kings 11:4 NKJV

For it was so, when Solomon was old, that his wives turned his heart after other gods; and his heart was not loyal to the Lord his God, as *was* the heart of his father David.

Malachi 3:6 NKJV

"For I *am* the Lord, **I do not change**.

Alcohol is a gift from God to be utilized in moderation. It is the drunkard that is the sin.

Genesis 14:18 NKJV

Then Melchizedek king of Salem brought out bread and wine; he *was* the priest of God Most High.

Genesis 27:28 NKJV

Therefore, may God give you of the dew of heaven, of the fatness of the earth, and plenty of grain and wine.

Leviticus 23:13 NKJV

Its grain offering *shall be* two-tenths *of an ephah* of fine flour mixed with oil, an offering made by fire to the Lord, for a sweet aroma; and its drink offering *shall be* of wine, one-fourth of a hin.

Numbers 15:10 NKJV

and you shall bring as the drink offering half a hin of wine as an offering made by fire, a sweet aroma to the Lord.

Deuteronomy 14:26 NKJV

And you shall spend that money for whatever your heart desires: for oxen or sheep, for wine or similar drink, for whatever your heart desires; you shall eat there before the Lord your God, and you shall rejoice, you and your household.

Matthew 11:18 NKJV

[18] For John came neither eating nor drinking, and they say, 'He has a demon.' [19] The Son of Man came eating and drinking, and they say, 'Look, a glutton and a winebibber, a friend of tax collectors and sinners!' But wisdom is justified by her children." [c]

John 2:6 NKJV

Now there were set there six water pots of stone, according to the manner of purification of the Jews, containing twenty or thirty gallons apiece. [7] Jesus said to them, "Fill the water pots with water." And they filled them up to the brim. [8] And He said to them, "Draw *some* out now, and take *it* to the master of the feast." And they took *it*. [9] When the master of the feast had tasted the water that was made wine and did not know where it came from (but the servants who had drawn the water knew), the master of the feast called the bridegroom. [10] And he said to him, "Every man at the beginning sets out the good wine, and when the *guests* have well drunk, then the inferior. You have kept the good wine until now!'"

Christ very 1st miracle...

1 Timothy 5:23 NKJV

No longer drink only water but use a little wine for your stomach's sake and your frequent infirmities.

Please do not tell me the wine back then was without alcoholic content for Noah was drunk, Lot could not even tell that was his own daughter or if he could, was so inebriated that he did not care, and I just can't see the guest at the wedding party being so ecstatic over the grape juice.

You do not go directly and immediately to heaven or hell when you die. You are asleep in the grave awaiting the rapture or you will rise at the "White Throne Judgment" and cast into the lake of fire.

Matthew 27:52 NKJV

and the graves were opened; and many bodies of the saints who had fallen asleep were raised.

Corinthians 15:20 NKJV

[20] But now Christ is risen from the dead and has become the first fruits of those who have fallen asleep.

1 Thessalonians 4:15 NKJV

For this we say to you by the word of the Lord, that we who are alive *and* remain until the coming of the Lord will by no means precede those who are asleep.

No one has ever been able to successfully give me a logical answer as to how the dead in Christ rise to meet him in the air if they are already with the Lord.?

There are 2 passages of scripture utilized to support that we have gone to heaven or hell immediately.

Luke 23:43 KJV (and 1599 Geneva)

43 Then Jesus said unto him, Verily I say unto thee, today <u>shalt</u> thou be with me in Paradise.

Luke 23:43 NKJV

43 And Jesus said to him, "Assuredly, I say to you, today you will be with Me in Paradise."

Earliest versions of the Bible & King James used the word "shalt" which is future tense while other later versions of various Bibles including the New King James have removed the word completely or use the word "shall", which I can see as being perceived as meaning "today", though I myself still see future tense no matter which word you use.

On that day, the thief obtained mercy and salvation and will see the Lord at the rapture. The thief is currently asleep in the grave. If you want to take it literally meaning on that very day, then you must ask where Christ was after his death on the cross. He was 3 days in the grave and then another 40 days with his disciples before ascending into heaven.

Did he tell the thief to go on ahead and I will catch up with you?

2 Corinthians 5:6 NKJV

Therefore, we are always bold, though we know that while we are at home in the body, we are absent from the Lord.

OK, so you assume that dead in the grave means absent from the body. Though you may be correct in your logic, we are not dead but simply asleep.

Later revisions of the Bible also appear to change the meaning of "Hades" referred to as a place of holding where all the dead went in early versions of the Bible and simply as Hell itself in later revisions.

More mass confusion due to simple word changes.

I can just envision the many mothers who have died and having left their children behind standing before the Lord just giving him eternal grief. He is not putting up with that! Now granted God may have pulled a few select individuals on into heaven to give a hand with preparations such as Enoch, but most of us, saved or unsaved are in a place of holding called "Hades", or asleep in the grave, awaiting the Rapture or the,

"White Throne Judgement."

Not everyone unsaved is going to suffer eternal torment in hell. They are simply burned up in the Lake of Fire. The Bible is very specific who suffers eternal torment.

Isaiah 53:5 NKJV

But He *was* wounded for our transgressions, *He was* bruised for our iniquities; the chastisement for our peace *was* upon Him, and by His stripes we are healed.

Luke 12:46 NKJV

[46] the master of that servant will come on a day when he is not looking for *him,* and at an hour when he is not aware, and will cut him in two and appoint *him* his portion with the unbelievers. [47] And that servant who knew his master's will and did not prepare *himself* or do according to his will, shall be beaten with many *stripes.* [48] But he who did not know, yet committed things deserving of stripes, shall be beaten with few. For everyone to whom much is given, from him much will be required; and to whom much has been committed, of him they will ask the more.

Revelation 14:11 NKJV

And the smoke of their torment ascends forever and ever; and they have no rest day or night, who worship the beast and his image, <u>and whoever receives the mark of his name</u>."

It is clear the Bible uses the term "stripes" as a metaphor for punishment. There will be a casting into the "Lake of Fire" for all unsaved. How long you live and suffer in the flames before your existence is extinguished will be the judgment of Jesus based on the severity of your sins. I would assume that it could be years or centuries before some debts are paid, before you no longer feel the pain, eventually left adrift, alone, in the darkness forever. It also makes it clear that those who knew the truth yet unsaved verses those who knew not will receive a greater length of time within the flames.

<u>Eternal torment</u> in hell's flames is reserved for the antichrist, beast, false prophet, and <u>all those who take the mark</u> of the beast.

Christ did not say "My God, My God why have you forsaken me" during his death on the cross.

Matthew 27:46 NKJV

And about the ninth hour Jesus cried out with a loud voice, saying, "<u>Eli, Eli,</u> lama sabachthani?" that is, "My God, My God, why have you forsaken me?"

God asking God why, God has forsaken God and especially relevant if your theology is the...

"All Knowing God" and/or that God is a single entity,

Has been one of the most mind blowing (for me at least) passages of scripture making absolutely no sense of which the masses have accepted without question.

Well, I have had questions!

Christ knew his purpose on earth and knew what was coming and being part of the Godhead knew of his resurrection to come. God knew God was not forsaking God! On that I can agree that God certainly knew.

One of the most profound and enlightening explanations I have heard was that of Eli, the name of the last high priest who allowed his sons to desecrate God's Temple. Jesus crying out on the cross was not directed at God but at his own people for admonishment. The commentator of this theory concluded that it was the point in time that God decided salvation would be offered to all people, for his own had rejected him despite having proven his love and power for them and through them repeatedly.

Those holding to the notion that the intent for Christ to come and die was the plan before creation wish to reference one passage of scripture.

Peter 1:19 NKJV

[19] but with the precious blood of Christ, as of a lamb without blemish and without spot. [20] He indeed was foreordained before the foundation of the world but was manifest in these last times for you [21] who through Him believe in God, who raised Him from the dead and gave Him glory, so that your faith and hope are in God.

Had the verse said "foreordained before the <u>creation</u> of the world" there might be no doubt, but the verse could also simply mean in front of or before, for all to see. It also could just be a reference to the fact Christ was foreordained as part of the God head in the beginning. It does not specifically say foreordained as a "sacrifice".

1 Samuel 2:12 NKJV

Now the sons of Eli *were* corrupt; they did not know the Lord.

1 Samuel 3:11 NKJV

[11] Then the LORD said to Samuel: "Behold, I will do something in Israel at which both ears of everyone who hears it will tingle. [12] In that day I will perform against Eli all that I have spoken concerning his house, from beginning to end. [13] For I have told him that I will <u>judge his house **forever**</u> for the iniquity which he knows, **because** <u>his sons made themselves vile</u>, and he did not restrain them. [14] **And therefore** <u>I have sworn to the house of Eli that the iniquity of Eli's house shall not be atoned for by sacrifice or offering forever."</u>

"<u>And therefore</u>" No longer will the killing of animals, or other sacrificial offerings be good enough to cover one's sins of which at that point in time only included God's chosen people. God himself will now come down in the form of a man and will be the final sacrifice for **all** who will believe in him "Christ".

The kingdom of Israel would later be destroyed with the kingdom of Judah soon to follow.

1 Samuel 4:10 NKJV

[10] So the Philistines fought, and Israel was defeated, and every man fled to his tent. There was a very great slaughter, and there fell of Israel thirty-thousand-foot soldiers. [11] Also the ark of God was captured; and the two sons of Eli, Hophni and Phinehas, died.

1 Samuel 4:18

Then it happened, when he made mention of the ark of God, that Eli fell off the seat backward by the side of the gate; and his neck was broken and he died, for the man was old and heavy. And he had judged Israel forty years.

Paul's "thorn in the flesh" was not a physical ailment but a sin he could not concur.

2 Corinthians 12:7 NKJV

[7] And lest I should be exalted above measure by the abundance of the revelations, a thorn in the flesh was given to me, a messenger of Satan to buffet me, lest I be exalted above measure. [8] Concerning this thing I pleaded with the Lord three times that it might depart from me. [9] And He said to me, "My grace is sufficient for you, for my strength is made perfect in weakness." Therefore, most gladly I will rather boast in my infirmities, that the power of Christ may rest upon me. [10] Therefore I take pleasure in infirmities, in reproaches, in needs, in persecutions, in distresses, for Christ's sake. For when I am weak, then I am strong.

Romans 7:14 NKJV

[14] For we know that the law is spiritual, but I am carnal, sold under sin. [15] For what I am doing, I do not understand. For what I will to do, that I do not practice; but <u>what I hate, that I do</u>. [16] If then, I do what I will not to do, I agree with the law that *it is* good.

Why does Paul need grace for a physical ailment?

We are the later day Babylon. It is "US"

Isaiah 21:6 NKJV

For thus has the Lord said to me:
"Go, set a watchman,
Let him declare what he sees."
[7] And he saw <u>a chariot</u> *with* a pair of horsemen,
<u>A chariot</u> of donkeys, *and* <u>a chariot</u> of camels, (3 planes)
And he listened earnestly with great care.
[8] Then he cried, "A lion,[a] my Lord!
I stand continually on the watchtower in the daytime;
I have sat at my post every night.
[9] And look, here comes a <u>chariot of men</u> *with* a <u>pair of horsemen</u>!"
(1st 2 of the 4 horseman)
Then he answered and said,
"Babylon is fallen, is fallen! (1, 2 towers)
And all the carved images of her gods (where world trade took place)
He has <u>broken to the ground</u>." (Both of them)
[13] <u>The burden against Arabia.</u> (Our response)
In the forest in Arabia you will lodge,
O you are traveling companies of Dedanites.
[14] O inhabitants of the land of Tema,
Bring water to him who is thirsty;
With their bread they met him who fled.
[15] For they fled from the swords, from the drawn sword,
From the bent bow, and from the distress of war.
[16] For thus the LORD has said to me: "Within a year, according
to the year of a hired man, all the glory of Kedar will fail; [17]
and the remainder of the number of archers, the mighty men of
the people of Kedar, will be diminished; for the LORD God of
Israel has spoken *it*."

The above is both actual history and metaphorical future prophesy on which most already agree.

You have seen the documentaries. The world changed on 9-11. It is the United States that has dominated the entire world. All trade between other countries since the end of WWII is in U.S. dollars and 9-11 was the start of the downfall of all the economies of the entire world. They have all been degrading ever since. What is coming will be a paperless money world economy whereas you will have to take that mark to live...

Revelation 13:7 NKJV

[7] It was also given to him to <u>make war with the [e]saints and to overcome them,</u> and authority over every tribe and people and tongue and nation was given to him. [8] All who dwell on the earth will worship him, *everyone* whose name has not been [f] <u>written from the foundation of the world</u> in the book of life of the Lamb who has been slain. [9] If anyone has an ear, let him hear. [10] If anyone [g]*is destined* for captivity, to captivity he goes; if anyone kills with the sword, with the sword he must be killed. Here is the [h]perseverance and the faith of the [i]saints.

Written from the foundation of the world does not imply that you were written in the book before creation ever started but simply that God has been writing in the book ever since the beginning of His creation and still is.

Revelation 13:17 NKJV

and *he provides* that no one will be able to buy or to sell, except the one who has the mark, *either* the name of the beast or the number of his name.

The Catholic Church was the first recognized Church. We Protestants were originally known as the "Protesters". It was when Martin Luther & his followers removed 7 books of the original Bible[1] and brought the world a "New Gospel" soon to be known as,

"King James".

If you have done any study of early Christianity, the proof is undeniable. It was what and is today's Catholic Church God utilized to assemble his word into a book to be delivered to all humanity and I am tired of listening to Protestant denominations <u>cult</u>ivating the Catholic Church. Baptists are the worst, with Catholics being their favorite target followed by Jehovah's Witnesses and Mormons. So, do you really think God would have used a cult to put together his word? I seriously doubt it. The early Protestant Church established by Martin Luther was known as "Protestors". Now I am in no way proclaiming the Catholic Church is the way to salvation even though they do have the most extravagant Cathedrals and I just love the architecture…

> [1]*Oxford Dictionary of Saints*
> Philip Hughes, *A history of the Church to the Eve of the Reformation.*
> J.M. Roberts, *The Penguin history of the World.*

1536	In his translation of the Bible from Greek into German, Luther removed 4 N.T. books (Hebrews, James, Jude, and Revelation) and placed them in an appendix saying they were less than canonical.

"Who so ever" says Christ, so your denomination does not matter.

Joel 2:32 NKJV

And it shall come to pass *that* <u>whoever</u> calls on the name of the Lord Shall be saved. For in Mount Zion and in Jerusalem there shall be deliverance, As the Lord has said, among the remnant whom the Lord calls.

Acts 2:21 NKJV

And it shall come to pass *that* whoever calls on the name of the Lord Shall be saved.'

Romans 10:13 NKJV

For "whoever calls on the name of the Lord shall be saved."

It does not say when Catholics or Baptists or Mormons call on the name of the Lord, <u>for that is the only thing that will save you</u>! The rest of your doctrine no matter what the denomination means nothing! What I never understood was how the Protestant Church concluded that merely saying you believe and walking up the aisle was going to be all that it took to reach salvation.

<u>Christ in no way alluded that you would not have to prove you believe</u>...

Christ message was plain and simple.

Mark 10:21 NKJV

Then Jesus, looking at him, loved him, and said to him, "One thing you lack: Go your way, sell whatever you have and give to the poor, and you will have treasure in heaven; and come, take up the cross, and follow me."

And for the next 400 years or so that is <u>exactly</u> what they did!

And then the message began to change…

2 Corinthians 11:4 NKJV

For if he who comes preaches another Jesus whom we have not preached, or *if* you receive a different spirit which you have not received, or a different gospel which you have not accepted— you may well put up with it!

Galatians 1:6 NKJV

I marvel that you are turning away <u>so soon</u> from Him who called you in the grace of Christ, to a different gospel, but even if we, or an angel from heaven, preach any other gospel to you than what we have preached to you, let him be accursed.

Once saved always saved. It is a commitment to be saved. You have not been guaranteed salvation just by walking up the aisle.

Exodus 32:33 NKJV

And the Lord said to Moses, "Whoever has sinned against Me, I will blot him out of my book.

Deuteronomy 9:14 NKJV

Let Me alone, that I may destroy them and blot out their name from under heaven; and I will make of you a nation mightier and greater than they.'

Revelation 3:5 NKJV

He who overcomes shall be clothed in white garments, and I will not blot out his name from the Book of Life; but I will confess his name before My Father and before His angels.

You have been written in the Book of Life upon your confession of faith, but your salvation has not been assured.

It is His book and though your name may be there you deceive yourself if you think He does not have the authority to erase it.

Most Christians are going to be tested to see if they are willing to die for Christ.

To live for Him is what you strive to do but fail.

You can actually do the other…

Satan was once <u>a son of God</u>, his creation and being a child was granted the <u>power of a God</u>. You would do the same for your child would you not? Having the power of a God, Satan no longer felt the need to be under the authority of God who had created him and rebelled, taking a 3rd of the angelic force with him. All angels have the <u>power of a God</u> and cannot be killed and there was "<u>War in Heaven</u>".

Imagine that! "War in Heaven" No wonder the earth has been at war for all creation. There is war in Heaven! I often wonder what if Satan had convinced more than half the angelic force. Why there would have been a coup in the Kingdom of God. Worse than that, if he had taken just half the angelic force, all creation would be at eternal war. Now I understand the justification for "Hell's Flames". The human race is replacement for the fallen angels but before God grants you the power of a god he is figuring out if He is going to be able to trust you are not. Are you going to love Him forever, your crown (your life with the power of a god) his to own and use or shall you be cast into the "Lake of Fire" where your mortal body and soul shall feel the flames, some for all eternity?

My understanding of "War" by shear definition would imply that there be an adversary capable of waging "War" or then it would be "War Games" …

I submit that the situation is a whole lot more serious than most imagine and there are "gods" at war! The God and creator of all there is and the gods whom he created whom have now rebelled.

God the creator seeks a family of his own to honor and love Him from amongst a family of gods all with the same powers their father has and now bestowed upon them by their father. God is not looking for robots or entities that have no choice but a family to love him because they want to. Salvation is the opportunity to join the family of God as a free willed god yourself casting your life (crown) at his feet.

I find the psychology of it all astounding for there will never be another rebellion in the Kingdom of God even though all of us will be of equal power and God like in nature. Creation finally at peace for all of eternity of which you will be a part. God the creator (all 3 of them) requires our respect and admiration for they are deserving of such and without it rebellion is a possibility. Bow before them while you still have time, or you will be cast out. There is no other solution to the problem caused by the 1st rebellion.

Genesis 2:8 NKJV

[8] The LORD God planted a garden eastward in Eden, and there He put the man whom He had formed. [9] And out of the ground the LORD God made every tree grow that is pleasant to the sight and good for food. The tree of life *was* also in the midst of the garden, and the tree of the knowledge of good and evil.

Genesis 3:22 NKJV

Then the LORD God said, "Behold, the man has become like one of us, to know good and evil. And now, <u>lest he put out his hand and take also of the tree of life, and eat, **and live forever**</u>"— [23] therefore the LORD God sent him out of the garden of Eden to till the ground from which he was taken. [24] So He drove out the man; and He placed cherubim at the east of the Garden of Eden, and a flaming sword which turned every way, to guard the way to the tree of life.

God removes Adam and Eve from the garden protecting the entrance to prevent them from eating of the tree of life or they would become immortal entities and could not be killed. Their existence was a test to see if they would be faithful before granting the gift of life everlasting. That is what Satan, and all angelic entities are, Immortals, meaning they cannot be killed and possess an

<u>"Angelic Faith"</u>

<u>"The ability to perform some tangible act at the speed of thought"</u>

Think not? You proclaim all the time how that must have been an angel that just saved you from the impending doom of the oncoming collision. Well, how do you think that angel performed such a task if it did not have the ability to perform some <u>tangible act at the speed of thought</u>?

Matthew 17:20 NKJV

So, Jesus said to them, "Because of your unbelief; for assuredly, I say to you, if you have faith as a mustard seed, you will say to this mountain, 'Move from here to there,' and it will move; **<u>and nothing will be impossible for you.</u>**

I call that a "god" I would not call it the "God" but I would call that a "god" and I have listened to a Baptist or two believing that you may have your own creative powers in Gods kingdom. Maybe…?

Now I call that a "god"

And you will be his "The Sole Creator of all Things" to use.

Genesis 6:1 NKJV

Now it came to pass, when men began to multiply on the face of the earth, and daughters were born to them, ² that the sons of God saw the daughters of men, that they *were* beautiful; and they took wives for themselves of all whom they chose. ³And the LORD said, My spirit shall not always strive with man, for that he also *is* flesh: yet his days shall be an hundred and twenty years.

A son of God is all angels.

Isaiah 14:13 NKJV

For you have said in your heart: 'I will ascend into heaven, I will exalt my throne above the stars of God; I will also sit on the mount of the congregation on the farthest sides of the north.

Luke 20:36 NKJV

nor can they die anymore, for they are equal to the angels and are sons of God, being sons of the resurrection.

James 1:12 NKJV

Blessed *is* the man who endures temptation; for <u>when</u> he has been approved, he will receive the <u>crown of life</u> which the Lord has promised to those who love Him.

Revelation 4:10 NKJV

The twenty-four elders fall down before Him who sits on the throne and worship Him who lives forever and ever, and<u> cast their crowns</u> before the throne

Cast their lives for him to use.

Revelation 12:7 NKJV

<u>And war broke out in heaven</u>: Michael and his angels fought with the dragon; and the dragon and his angels fought,

Surly if <u>that</u> were to be a parable or metaphor it would have been noted as such like all the others. For it to mean anything other than <u>exactly what it says</u> sends my head in a tail spin, for there is no logical explanation other than I have the "Holy Spirit" and it means x, y, or z.

You whom even try to explain it simply say that I have no idea what that means, and you can't come up with an x, a y or a z, though you proclaim the "Holy Spirit".

My favorite quote from Christians

"We're just not meant to understand the mind of God."

You're right! When I read the Bible from the perspective of the all-knowing God, **nothing makes any sense.**

<u>**There's no understanding to be had!**</u>

And thus, is the reason you believe x, y or z...?

The reason you believe x, y or z is because that is what you were taught. People in general and for the most part simply believe what they get taught. Few will change during one's life. Once having been taught and believe there is nothing you read from the Bible that you do not end up reconciling in some way to coincide with your pre-conceived beliefs.

Corinthians 14:33 NKJV

For <u>God is not *the author* of confusion</u> but of peace, as in all the churches of the saints.

The generations of Christians at the end of this story are dying for their faith. It does not matter the denomination. Put your faith in the name of "Jesus" and the world is going to kill you. You and your family will die for him. The rest of your doctrine will mean nothing

Narrow is the road...

Matthew 7:14 NKJV

Because narrow *is* the gate and <u>difficult *is* the way</u> which leads to life, <u>and there are few who find it</u>.

Luke 9:24 NKJV

For whoever desires to save his life will lose it, but <u>whoever loses his life for my sake will save it</u>.

Protestants twist this one verse more than any other implying that it means to live your life free of sin of which none of us are capable of...

I say it means <u>exactly what it says</u>.

Luke 13:24 NKJV

"Strive to enter through the narrow gate, for many, I say to you, will <u>seek to enter and will not be able</u>.

Philippians 1:29 NKJV

For to you it has been granted on behalf of Christ, not only to believe in Him, <u>but also to suffer for His sake</u>

1 Thessalonians 3:4 NKJV

For, in fact, we told you before when we were with you that <u>we would suffer tribulation</u>, just as it happened, and you know.

2 Thessalonians 1:5 NKJV

which is manifest evidence of the righteous judgment of God, that you may be counted <u>worthy of the kingdom of God, for which you also suffer.</u>

2 Thessalonians 2:2 NKJV

2 Now, brethren, concerning the coming of our Lord Jesus Christ and our gathering together to Him, we ask you, [2] not to be soon shaken in mind or troubled, either by spirit or by word or by letter, as if from us, as though the day of Christ[a] had come. [3] Let no one deceive you by any means; for *that Day will not come* <u>unless the falling away comes first</u>, and the man of sin[b] is

revealed, the son of perdition, ⁴ who opposes and exalts himself above all that is called God or that is worshiped, so that he sits as God[c] in the temple of God, showing himself that he is God

The rapture does not take place until the antichrist is revealed. The falling away are those who have professed Christ but will end up taking the mark because they are unwilling to die for him where upon your name will be blotted out of the book and your eternal tormented future assured.

1 Peter 3:14 NKJV

But even if you should suffer for righteousness' sake, *you are* blessed. "And do not be afraid of their threats, nor be troubled."

Romans 8:17 NKJV

and if children, then heirs—heirs of God and joint heirs with Christ, if indeed we suffer with *Him, that we may also be glorified together.*

Romans 8:31 NKJV

³¹ What then shall we say to these things? If God *is* for us, who *can be* against us? ³² He who did not spare His own Son, but delivered Him up for us all, how shall He not with Him also freely give us all things? ³³ Who shall bring a charge against God's elect? *It is* God who justifies. ³⁴ Who *is* he who condemns? *It is* Christ who died, and furthermore is also risen, who is even at the right hand of God, who also makes intercession for us. ³⁵ Who shall separate us from the love of Christ? *Shall* tribulation, or distress, or persecution, or famine, or nakedness, or peril, or sword? ³⁶ As it is written:

**"For Your sake we are killed all day long;
We are accounted as sheep for the slaughter."**

2 Timothy 3:12 NKJV

Yes, and all who desire to live godly <u>in Christ</u> Jesus <u>will suffer
persecution</u>.

Revelation 2:10 NKJV

Do not fear any of those things which you are about to suffer.
Indeed, the devil is about to throw *some* of you into prison, that
you may be tested, and you will have tribulation ten days. <u>Be
faithful until death, and I will give you the crown of life.</u>

Revelation 3:5 NKJV

<u>He who overcomes</u> shall be clothed in white garments, **and I
will not blot out his name from the Book of Life**; but I will
confess his name before My Father and before His angels.

Revelation 6:9 NKJV

[9] When He opened the fifth seal, I saw under the altar <u>the souls
of those who had been **slain**</u> for the word of God and for the
testimony which they held. [10] And they cried with a loud voice,
saying, "How long, O Lord, holy and true, until you judge and
avenge our blood on those who dwell on the earth?" [11] Then **a
white robe** was given to each of them; and it was said to them
that they should rest a little while longer, until both *the number
of* their fellow servants and their brethren, **who would be killed
as they** *were*, was completed.

Revelation 7:9 NKJV

After these things I looked, and behold, a great multitude which no one could number, of all nations, tribes, peoples, and tongues, standing before the throne and before the Lamb, **clothed with white robes,** with palm branches in their hands, [10] and crying out with a loud voice, saying, "Salvation *belongs* to our God who sits on the throne, and to the Lamb!" [11] All the angels stood around the throne and the elders and the four living creatures, and fell on their faces before the throne and worshiped God, [12] saying:

"Amen! Blessing and glory and wisdom,

Thanksgiving and honor and power and might,

Be to our God forever and ever.

Amen."

[13] Then one of the elders answered, saying to me, "Who are these arrayed in white robes, and where did they come from?"

[14] And I said to him, "Sir,[b] you know."

So, he said to me, "These are the ones who come out of the great tribulation and **washed their robes and made them white in the blood of the Lamb.** [15] Therefore they are before the throne of God and serve Him day and night in His temple. And He who sits on the throne will dwell among them. [16] They shall neither hunger anymore nor thirst anymore; the sun shall not strike them, nor any heat; [17] for the Lamb who is in the midst of the throne will shepherd them and lead them to living fountains of waters. [c] And God will wipe away every tear from their eyes."

Revelation 13:15 NKJV

[15] He was granted *power* to give breath to the image of the beast, that the image of the beast should both speak <u>and cause as many as would not worship the image of the beast to be killed</u>. [16] He causes all, both small and great, rich and poor, free and slave, <u>to receive a mark</u> on their right hand or on their foreheads, [17] <u>and that no one may buy or sell except one who has the mark</u> or[f] the name of the beast, or the number of his name.

Revelation 14:8 NKJV

[8] And another angel followed, saying, "Babylon[a] is fallen, is fallen, that great city, because she has made all nations drink of the wine of the wrath of her fornication."

[9] Then a third angel followed them, saying with a loud voice, "If anyone worships the beast and his image, and receives *his* mark on his forehead or on his hand, [10] he himself shall also drink of the wine of the wrath of God, which is poured out full strength into the cup of His indignation. He shall be tormented with fire and brimstone in the presence of the holy angels and in the presence of the Lamb.

In regard to all fellow believers in Christ who have gone on before without actually having died for him.,

Salvation lies in the hands of Jesus. It is simply His judgment call...

I have no idea if they have been saved or not.

As for myself, my earnest prayer these days has been.

"Please oh Lord, allow both my angels to remain close to me though my sins are many. I beg you for the forgiveness of those sins and hope that there not be another of greater value to you in your kingdom that my protection is of greater value elsewhere...

I beg you oh Lord to please keep me alive not only that I may live for you (the best I can) but to protect me until the day cometh that...

"I May Die for You!!!"

THE ULTIMATE ACT OF FAITH

It's an awesome story!!! The depths of which most fail to comprehend...

Now God's address to the 7 churches indicates there are two he is happy with so in all fairness to those of you holding fast to your doctrine in the hope that you belong to the Church of Philadelphia of which God does appear to indicate that you will not be persecuted like the Church of Smyrna, I concede the possibility of a pre-trib rapture, or simply a quick easy death which might consist of those in the last days whom upon their justification or commitment to be saved that their walk was pure and sins after their justification were few and trivial.

Of which sadly, mine are not...

I do not think it will be a church of denomination based on their doctrine otherwise upon all I have ever read and observed during my pathetic walk with Christ, I would be inclined to convert to Catholicism. If only they did not make it such a struggle.

And no church is going to be able to tell me they have the power to annul my 1st marriage in order to wipe away the sin, and thus the children must not be, or that would be sin as well.,

Or is it you have the authority to wipe them away as well?

The Persecuted Church

Revelation 2:8 NKJV

[8] "And to the angel of the church in Smyrna write,

'These things says the First and the Last, who was dead, and came to life: [9] "I know your works, tribulation, and poverty (but you are rich); and *I know* the blasphemy of those who say they are Jews and are not, but *are* a synagogue of Satan. [10] Do not fear any of those things which you are about to suffer. Indeed, the devil is about to throw *some* of you into prison, that **you may be tested**, and you will have tribulation ten days. **Be faithful until death,** and I will give you the **crown of life.**

The Faithful Church

Revelation 3:7 NKJV

[7] "And to the angel of the church in Philadelphia write,

'These things says He who is holy, He who is true, "He who has the key of David, He who opens and no one shuts, and shuts and no one opens":[c] [8] "I know your works. See, I have set before you an open door, and no one can shut it;[d] for you have a little strength, have kept My word, and have not denied My name. [9] Indeed I will make *those* of the synagogue of Satan, who say they are Jews and are not, but lie—indeed I will make them come and worship before your feet, and to know that I have loved you. [10] Because you have kept My command to persevere, I also will keep you from the hour of trial which shall come upon the whole world, to test those who dwell on the earth. [11] Behold, [e] I am coming quickly! Hold fast what you have, that no one may take your crown. [12] He who overcomes, I will make him a pillar in the temple of My God, and he shall go out no more. I will write on him the name of My God and the name of the city of My God, the New Jerusalem, which comes down out of heaven from My God. And *I will write on him* My new name.

One of God's sons' rebels, takes a 3rd of all the angelic force with him, and there was,

"War in Heaven"

Now I understand the mind of God…

He is angry!!!

And it is not because that it was his will…

Revelation 8 thru 17 NKJV

The first angel sounded: And hail and fire followed, mingled with blood, and they were thrown to the earth. And a third of the trees were burned up, and all green grass was burned up.

Then the second angel sounded: And *something* like a great mountain burning with fire was thrown into the sea, and a third of the sea became blood.

And a third of the living creatures in the sea died, and a third of the ships were destroyed.

Then the third angel sounded: And a great star fell from heaven, burning like a torch, and it fell on a third of the rivers and on the springs of water.

The name of the star is Wormwood. <u>A third</u> of the waters became wormwood, and many men died from the water, because it was made bitter.

Then the fourth angel sounded: And <u>a third</u> of the sun was struck, a third of the moon, and <u>a third</u> of the stars, so that <u>a third</u> of them were darkened. <u>A third</u> of the day did not shine, and likewise the night.

So, the four angels, who had been prepared for the hour and day and month and year, were released to kill <u>a third</u> of mankind.

By these three *plagues* <u>a third</u> of mankind was killed—by the fire and the smoke and the brimstone which came out of their mouths.

His tail drew <u>a third</u> of the stars of heaven and threw them to the earth. And the dragon stood before the woman who was ready to give birth, to devour her Child as soon as it was born.

So, the great dragon was cast out, that serpent of old, called the Devil and Satan, who deceives the whole world; he was cast to the earth, and his angels were cast out with him.

Then <u>a third</u> angel followed them, saying with a loud voice, "If anyone worships the beast and his image, and receives *his* mark on his forehead or on his hand…

[signature]

9-11-2013

10-29-2013

My final thoughts…

Hear the words of the false prophets as the world governments begin to implant you with that mark, one of which appears to have started some 400 years after the death and resurrection of the Lord Jesus Christ.

- "Have no fear, for it is not the mark, for if it were the mark, you would not be here."
- "He died for you; you do not have to die for him"
- "Trust us, Jesus is coming and will be here soon"

And it won't be until it actually looks you in the face and says,

"I am God!"

Before you're gonna realize, you should have gone ahead and checked on out with the other brothers and sisters in Christ who have left already, while you sat there all comfy waiting on your,

"RAPTURE"!

11/4/2013

I lied!

And I'm going to continue my thoughts here as I continue to dwell on it all...

It did not hit me till I wrote it all down and I cannot speak for the Catholics since I have not been around them other than to go to a few services to see what was up. It was enlightening to sit through one and take part in the prayer being blasted by the Protestants that the Catholics are praying to Mary. They are praying to Jesus and are simply asking Mary to please join them in their prayer to her son. It is no different than you are asking your fellow congregation to join you in your prayer or asking another for their prayers for your problems. I would ask her as well if I believed she was there and could actually hear me, but I have no idea if Jesus has pulled her up to Heaven yet or if she has been left peacefully sleeping.

And now that I have my rant going, another favorite of the Protestants is this bit about the fact Catholics go through a Priest to confess their sins. The Protestant proclaims, "You don't need an intercessor. You can speak directly to Jesus to confess your sins!" Easy enough but to have to confess your sins to another congregation member and especially if the sins would embarrass you takes much more humility and effort on one's part and is instructed by God to do so, that you are indeed to confess to another. At least the Catholics have set up some system for you to go tell someone. Who are you telling?

James 5:16 NKJV

Confess *your* trespasses to one another, and pray for one another, that you may be healed. The effective, fervent prayer of a righteous man avails much.

And please, you can keep your "Anger" or "Obesity" sin. The only one a Protestant will dare confess to and only because it is obvious. Unless you took God's name in vain or killed someone during your anger I am not impressed. If that is all the sin you have going on you certainly deserve to be raptured…

The fact is you are, a "Tea Totting Thief" while criticizing the Catholic hierarchy for sending their flock a bill for the 10% they owe while we steel from God every week, your greatest achievement being the fact you don't drink.

Please, it's not even within the top ten…

I remember when I finally finished reading that story and the only thought going through my mind was…

"Wow! These people are going to "<u>Die!</u>" <u>for this Man</u>!

Well, I'm not getting left behind…"

"Somebody get me a beer!"

Up the aisle I went, only to find out the masses are going "Huh?

"We're getting "Raptured."

Get off um! Those people were dying for their faith to get Gods word out to all of humanity at the start of it all only to end up being lambasted by the "Protestors".

Yeah, your right, having to actually "<u>Die</u>" for the Man when you were not there is a bit much to have to accept and it looks like the later day Catholic Church is also deceived for neither do, they preach you have to "<u>Die for Christ</u>".

Though I think they know and just do not want to talk about it.

I just wonder what the ratio is of Catholics verses Protestants in the mission fields doing just that.

My bet is on the Catholics!

And I would like some real wine for my "Communion" for once!

I now believe the entire Protestant faith of all denominations and possibly the Catholics as well have all been deceived for the last 1,600 plus years and you literally have had to "<u>Die for Christ</u>" to be saved…

Yeah, there are few that have found that door. Very few!

Note those in the final book who are dressed in "**<u>White Robes</u>**".

There are <u>none</u> noted who were not <u>slain!</u>

It is easy to comprehend wanting to die for him. Imagine if you had been there at the time. Life was hard then! Nowhere near all the modern conveniences you have now and along comes this man performing all these miracles, dies, rises, tells his people, if you want to be like me, grab your cross and follow...

If you had actually seen it and heard it there would be no doubt and you would be running looking for some soul to tell all about Jesus just hoping they make your death quick and easy, of which there is no guarantee.

Might just depend on the depth of your sins or if Jesus still requires your services.

You will just have to ask him if you get there.

I have no idea and am simply throwing ideas out there.

Wish I had been there...

11/5/2013

Your Gods, the ones in charge are just that and I found it confusing how things seemed so cut and dry within the Protestant beliefs such as simply coming forth seeking forgiveness to be saved, or Heaven & Hell being one way or the other.

I find that Father, Son, and Holy Ghost are Judge and Jury and what ends up happening to you and/or yours, is in their hands and their hands only. You have no say in the matter and will be content that you are alive though your loved ones may be elsewhere. And elsewhere is wherever God, Son & Holy Ghost after having dwelt over you and discussed it amongst themselves have decided it shall be. And the temperatures vary, for a flaming bottomless pit, its mouth the Lake of Fire is eternally deep, and they will simply stop you somewhere along the timeline for you to finish out your sentence, probably all alone where you will sit there on your knees, some for all eternity, your face in your hands, and dwelling only on God. For if you move you sink just a bit and it just gets hotter.

Kind of like boiling quicksand or something...

As for Satan and his angelic followers though they may be immune to the pain being immortal entities and all, shall in the end, will have been contained at least and an eternal fall down some pit like that must at least work on the mind…

You will be one tormented soul even if you are a "god"

The other side to that coin for those who have made it, your life will be judged in total by the Three. Christ the Son had sole decision on if you got through the door, not a door, but the door. And the rewards will vary. Some will be sitting on nice pasture and some will be serving those sitting on the nice pasture. You're just glad to be alive! Something tells me David will probably be serving Uriah. I know he best have one sincere apology for him once he sees him. The pasture is out there before you. My favorite thought I have heard from others (those on the nice pasture) (Stars) in reality their own planet to create whatever they desire after a review from the "Board of Three". Submit your plans, get their stamp of approval, and go for it. And there will be those who are serving those who are creating it all, and the scientist say the heavens appear to be never ending.

So, you're a slave! Who cares, you are just glad to be alive!

My point in the above metaphorical fantasy or not is though my message throughout appears bleak, for I feel like some kind of modern-day Moses and have been battling keeping this to myself for 30 years or so, for people do not want to hear what I have had to say, for I have been saying it since first having read the story.

"Lord", I can't go tell these people that"

My mama went off one day, "You can't tell people that! They can't take it! We're getting raptured!"

And I have been ever since amongst you listening to all you have had to say keeping my own opinions fairly low key though everyone knew I was different. The "odd ball" they called me. You were right. I did not get taught.

I simply read the story, exactly as written, and in the order, it was assembled.

And the final point was? There is not cut and dry on who has been saved. There is the Church of Philadelphia, and the Bible is clear that not all shall see death. If one truly believed in their heart and their life changed, sins being few and trivial after their conversion than "Jesus" a just and righteous God will have sole discretion on if you come through the door or not. Some get in, some do not. So, let me remain clear. I do not believe we will <u>all</u>, or those who have gone on before us have had to <u>all</u>, literally "<u>Die for Christ</u>", for us <u>all</u>, to be saved.

But if you want the guarantee, come on in, no questions asked, you need to check out those wearing the…

"**White Robes**"

In the meantime, best be working on keeping those lust at bay for saved or not your rewards and/or punishment is going to vary.

For those of you and there are a bunch of Baptists in this boat since having berated your children to get on up there and "Be Saved" at the age of 6, their sins after their conversion many and never ending which is not much different than the Catholics & Lutherans sprinkling the water over the baby.

All have another chance coming. You want to be saved you will…

"**Die for Christ**"!

The communion cup was the reason my children went forward. Passing the cup by them having to let them know they cannot have any till they go and get saved and up they went.

"Jesus? Yeah, yeah, yeah, I know Jesus, pass the cup!"

You could have at least had some real wine in it!

Just call me "Moses Friar Tuck" I kind of like that…

I have never made much attempt to try and talk to people about Christ because I felt the need to be sure to let them know "Welcome Aboard" this is the "Titanic" if there ever was one but without the life boats.

"Prepare to rise as a "god"

No point in keeping them in the dark for that would be misleading…

It just did not jive with anyone.

And I couldn't understand why, for who would not want to rise as a "god"?

Kidding aside, for this reality is no joke and I am laughing and crying like never before for this is serious stuff going down and nobody seems to see it coming but me,

as you prepare to fly away…

"KUM BA YA"

You're so deceived…

Do not tell my children they are getting "Raptured". I prefer they believe they will die for Him if need be and if found worthy to escape the testing than "PRAISE GOD". I just don't want to see them totally devastated when the truth is finally figured out that you are indeed going to die for the Man, and to perhaps watch your families die for the Man, and that they will understand the reasons why.

Humanity dies daily, some in the most horrendous ways and for absolutely no purpose at all. At least to die for "Christ" has some purpose and meaning and reward. What are we waiting for? Every day we wait we strengthen the odds that we will die for nothing.

I would not teach "Predestination" to my children even if I believed it to be true. They can just wait to hear that one once they get there. Predestination takes away all desire to care if you are saved or lost for it does not matter since nothing you do would change the outcome. You can have your cake and eat it too. No real change in the consequence for your sin or reward for your effort. Nothing changes. Why would you care?

I penned this below not long after my conversion years ago.

My disdain for so called religious holidays is noted. Mother's at her worst.

Easter, I find to be the most bizarre as people go find a place outside somewhere to worship the rising son.

"Christ has risen, time to hide bunny eggs"

I just know Jesus is proud…

Smokin Chimney

For Behold, What Do I See

Green Eyed Gremlin

Perched upon Santa's Sleigh

Stolen from the Pain Fields

Rubbing the Polished Red Nose of his Little Wooden Reindeer

GRANT ME MY WISHES! Screams the Gremlin!

Silence Fills the Air

The Gremlin Enraged Screams Again

GRANT ME MY WISHES NOW!!!

Still the Little Wooden Reindeer Remains Silent, It's Gaze Affixed on the Stars Beyond

The Gremlin More Angered Now than Ever, Squeezing and Shaking His Little Wooden IDOL

GRANT ME MY WISHES NOW, OR I'LL THROW YOU DOWN THE SMOKIN CHIMNEY!!!

In the Twinkling of an Eye the Little Wooden Reindeer Springs to Life

"YOUR THREE WISHES LAY WITHIN THE THREE BAGS OF WHICH YOU ARE PEARCHED UPON"

YEAHHHAHHAH!!! Wild Eyed Fool Flings the Little Reindeer into the Stars

It's Nose Flashing in Surprise

And Plunges His Fanged Claws into the Bags Beneath Him

Just as Quickly as They Went In, does he Drag Them Out

Throwing the Contents Wildly into the Wind

A White Powder Flies through the Air

Settling in Over the Gremlin and Santa's Sleigh…

"AHHHH! THE SNOW…

I JUST LOVE THE SNOW"

And the Gremlin Falls back into his Comfy Bags Sliding off into a Deep Sleep

No Sooner had the Gremlin Gone to sleep that He Awakes

Sleigh Plunging out of Control

The Little Wooden Reindeer, No longer there to Guide It

Green Eyes Wide and Screaming in Horror!

AAAAAAGGAAGAAAAAHHH!!! SMOKIN CHIMNEY!!!

Before Time to Jump, Santa's Sleigh Slams

Bricks Blasting into the Blue

Sleigh Plunging through One Way and Non-Stop

Force so Great, Tree and Presents Gone

Down into the Fiery Bottomless Pit

Green Eyed Gremlin Close Behind

Claws dug into the Sides of the Molten Chimney

Desperately Trying not to Sink Further

Fangs Slowly Melt Away

NOOOOOOOOOOOOOOOOOOOOOOOOOOOOOOOOOOOOOOOO OOOOOO.......

And as the Screams Begin to Fade

The Children Awake

Crying to their Father about the Terrible Nightmare They Had Just Witnessed

Gathering Them in His Arms

Wiping the Tears from Their Eyes

Leading them to the Presents He has Prepared

The Father Lets Them Know

"GREEN-EYED GREMLIN IS GONE AND THERE IS NOTHING TO FEAR ANYMORE"

11/7/2013

I AM THAT I AM or was THAT WHO I AM?

One of the most profound statements within the Bible.

<u>I AM THAT I AM</u>

I smiled when I first read it picturing the not all-knowing God saying what he said while thinking to himself.

"It's a Mystery my Son; All I know is that "I AM THAT I AM"

Now I just don't know what to think. Truly lost trying to figure the "Mind of God", on this one and only because someone along the way felt the need to re-write the story.

I liked what I read the first time and don't know what to think of

"WHO", or was that "WHAT"?

Yeah, somebody's next revision I'm sure.

"I AM WHAT I AM."

Exodus 3:14 1599 Geneva Bible

14 And God answered Moses, I AM THAT I AM. Also he said, Thus shalt thou say unto the children of Israel, I AM hath sent me unto you.

Exodus 3:14 KJV

14And God said unto Moses, I AM THAT I AM: and he said, Thus shalt thou say unto the children of Israel, I AM hath sent me unto you.

Exodus 3:14 NKJV

14 And God said to Moses, "I AM WHO I AM." And He said, "Thus you shall say to the children of Israel, 'I AM has sent me to you.' "

Exodus 3:13 NKJV

¹³ Moses said to God, "Suppose I go to the Israelites and say to them, 'The God of your fathers has sent me to you,' and they ask me, 'What is his name?' Then what shall I tell them?"

See there, Moses had it right to begin with and should have just said "Yes", when they asked, "What is his name"?

And thus, is the reason for so much confusion over the "Mind of God" and the reason why everyone needs to get off everyone's case.

All denominations need to cease with the...

"**We** are The Way, The Truth and The Light"

Because there is but one way and you are **all** in the same boat.

JC TITANIC

Unless you are already walking on water, I would start to prepare your heart and mind to go on down with the rest of us...

Rise as a "god"

And Fly Away...

3/19/2014

Source: Wikipedia

On 31 October 1517, Luther posted the ninety-five theses, which he had composed in Latin, on the door of the Castle Church of Wittenberg, according to university custom.

John 10:9 NKJV

I am **the** door. If anyone enters by me, he will be saved, and will go in and out and find pasture.

Notice Luther did not go through the door.

Perhaps he should have just gone on in to chat a bit to address those issues that plagued him.

Instead, he put a nail in it and walked away.

And the date is more than fitting…

"God Bless!!!"

Printed in the United States
by Baker & Taylor Publisher Services